INWARD TO THE BONES

INWARD TO THE BONES

Georgia O'Keeffe's Journey with Emily Carr

Kate Braid

POLESTAR
BOOK PUBLISHERS

Polestar Book Publishers acknowledges the ongoing support of The Canada Council for the Arts, the British Columbia Arts Council, and the Department of Canadian Heritage.

The cover photograph is "On the Portal, Ghost Ranch, 1959" by Todd Webb, used with the kind permission of the Evans Gallery, Portland, Maine.
Cover design by Val Speidel
Printed and bound in Canada

Earlier versions of some of these poems were originally printed by (m)Other Tongue Press in 1997, as part of their National Chapbook contest and by *The Canadian Forum* (July/August 1997).

The "found" poems on pages 14, 17, 21, 24, 25, 29 and 115 were fashioned from lines and phrases in the letters of Georgia O'Keeffe to Anita Pollitzer (copyright held by The Georgia O'Keeffe Foundation, 1988). They are reprinted here by kind permission of The Georgia O'Keeffe Foundation and Donald Gallup, agent for the Stieglitz/O'Keeffe archive in the Yale Collection of American Literature.

CANADIAN CATALOGUING IN PUBLICATION
Braid, Kate, 1947-
Inward to the bones
ISBN 1-896095-40-2
I. O'Keeffe, Georgia, 1887-1986 — Poetry.   2. Carr, Emily,
1871-1945 — Poetry.   I. Title
PS8553.R2585I5 1998 C811'.54   C98-910144-4
PR9199.3.B677I5 1998

Library of Congress Card Catalog Number: 98-84380

Polestar Book Publishers   In the United States:
P.O. Box 5238, Station B   Polestar Book Publishers
Victoria, British Columbia   P.O. Box 468
Canada   V8R 6N4   Custer, WA
http://mypage.direct.ca/p/polestar/   USA   98240-0468

5 4 3 2 1

INWARD TO THE BONES
GEORGIA O'KEEFFE'S JOURNEY WITH EMILY CARR

In February 1930, the Canadian artist Emily Carr met the American artist Georgia O'Keeffe. The meeting occurred at Alfred Stieglitz' gallery, An American Place, in New York City, where O'Keeffe was having an exhibition. At the time, Georgia O'Keeffe was forty-three years old and Emily Carr was fifty-nine. Emily, in her extensive journals, mentions it only in passing and speaks more about one of the paintings (*The D.H. Lawrence Tree*) than about Georgia herself. Georgia mentions it not at all.

To me, this passing incident was a spark that struck fire. Here were two of the great abstract painters of the 20th century — among the very few women of the time with a commitment to being artists. What if they had caught each other's attention? Would they have travelled together, perhaps? If so, of course they would have gone to New Mexico and British Columbia, the places so vital to each of them.

No sooner had I thought of them travelling, than they were off. I could hardly keep up. The first eleven poems came spilling out within a week — in the voice of Georgia O'Keeffe.

This has been a fascinating journey. I have tried to keep as closely as possible to Georgia O'Keeffe's real (or at least, "reported") life. There was a romance and mystique to O'Keeffe's life from the very first, and it continued until she died, at the age of ninety-eight, in 1986. So the incidents explored in the poems and noted in the back of this book probably happened, and if they didn't — well, they might have. I have also included some quotes from her letters, in the form of "found" poems. Georgia O'Keeffe shared with Emily Carr a writing style that was as exciting and as unconventional as the rest of her life. I thank her for taking me on this trip, for allowing me to record it. Also, my thanks to Emily. Again.

I would like to give special thanks to Shauna Fowler for helping me articulate my instinct and urging me to keep faith with it, and to George McWhirter in the Creative Writing program at the University of British Columbia, who taught me word magic.

Thanks also to Keith Maillard and to Marilyn Dumont, Veronica Gaylie, Miranda Pearson, Denise Ryan, Sandy Shreve and Esta Spalding, each of whom entered these poems with me; Nicola Aime, who brought me a poem from South Africa; Nancy Hannum, who kept me supplied with books and belief; David Carlin, who offered musical accompaniment; Paul and Monica Petrie and Anne Cameron, who provided shelter; Susan Crean, who shares my excitement about these two women; and Joy Kogawa, who assured me it is okay just to honour the question. And this book wouldn't exist without Beverley Richardson asking the question — "What do you really want?" — that sent me back to UBC and the MFA in Creative Writing that was the foundation for this manuscript.

And, as always, my love and thanks to John Steeves, who continues to believe.

The distance has always been calling me ...
— *Georgia O'Keeffe*

I. SOLO

But even a woman cannot live only into the distance.
— *D.H. Lawrence*

1.

My first memory is of colour. I remember mother's
dress, red with white polka-dot bubbles. When mother
rose and walked away, I wanted to hold red.

Later, she sent me for lessons with Mrs. Mann.
I dipped my paintbrush — strange stick — into a bath
of brilliant orange, splashed it over paper and watched
colour come alive. I built landscapes and figures.
Mama was clear red. I was yellow.

Mrs. Mann said I was gifted. She said Mama must
send me again. I said yes. I had learned the power
of the sun — to shine.

I did not like the teacher's dog, large and smelly.
When Mrs. Mann looked away I touched him with
my orange brush. He growled. I retreated. When I put
my brush on paper, I painted a huge brown beast with
claws and a muzzle that glowed. The animal stood back
panting, obedient to my wishes — drooled, orange.

2.

When visitors came, Mama hid me
in the back parlour, judged
my pockmarked skin
too ugly to be seen.

I was the unfavoured child,
left in the twilight
anticipating independence
like a gift on Christmas Eve.

It was all right — I amused myself,
projecting lines against dusky white walls.
Blank as canvas, I dreamed
in colour.

3.

While Mama minded the house
and Auntie, the other children,
while Papa ran the farm,
I took my own family
to the garden.

I had them all —
tiny wooden figures of mother, father, child,
a house I constructed
from two pieces of wood,
a cardboard cow,
a bowl of water for the lake.

Here was my world, mirror
in which I alone
decided the order of life, the fate
of my small but perfect family.

4.

The year I was finishing eighth grade
I said very definitely to the washerwoman's daughter,
One day I am going to be an artist.
I don't really know where I got my artist idea.
Maybe it was the small drawing I found
of a girl — in ordinary pen-and-ink — two
    inches high.
For me, it was something special — so beautiful.
The title under it was: "Maid of Athens."
I believe that picture started something moving in me,
something that kept on going and had to do
with this everlasting urge
that makes me keep on painting.

(found poem)

5.

Loose black dresses (a lady doesn't wear pants),
my hair in a bun, never bobbed,
the world flowed past me casting up
short skirts, red lips
only to ebb again.

What could I possibly have painted
if I were dressed in red?
I would not be distracted,
saved all my adornment for the pictures.

6.

My teachers said, *A composition must be beautiful.*
It is one of the few rules I have never broken.

I worked without the usual feminine accoutrements,
took the fiercer path of black and white.

Oxfords, tailored suits and simple lines
filled my light and dark —

the white glare of the paper —
beautifully.

7.

I had been taught to work like others
and after careful thinking I decided
I wasn't going to spend my life doing
what had already been done.

I decided to start anew —
to strip away what I had been taught —
to accept as true my own thinking.
I was alone and singularly free
working into my own unknown.

(found poem)

8.

I simplified,
painted my life in black and white,
saved all colour
for the paintings. Even my room
was white. On its snow-driven walls I hung
a square of plain black cloth in a plain black frame
and there I rested my eyes.
(Oh blackness, save me!)
Other than that, I lived
as others expected me.

The broad hand of Stieglitz
outstretched from New York
was the only offer of interest. Even then,
I thought that when he really knew me,
he would despise the woman I am,
who took it.

9.

I was always afraid and yet
I carried on because to stop
as I did in Chicago, to make my living drawing
lace collars or nursing mother, was to die
as she did, slowly.
Anything was better
than a life without canvas or colour.
Is there such a word as *freeest*?
Free-est.

10.

If I was to see with a clear eye
for a long time, over distance,
I had to guard myself
from feeling.

It is why I lived alone, doled out love
in small, brilliant daubs,
hoarded my feelings, saved them
for the pictures,
where I wanted everyone
to love me.

11.

Stieglitz has been writing me.
Yesterday he told me
that he had taken down my things
and the place is empty.
But his letters —
they have been like fine cold water
when you are terribly thirsty.

(found poem)

12.

Georgia O'Keeffe —

he wrote it like a love poem. Already
he loved my name. He wrote it
as one day I would write myself,
so like him I would become —

resisting all the way.

13.

I was large, lean and long like a birch trunk — my
hands especially. I pushed into this world hands first,
moved from one room to another, my hands
outstretched. Hot. Cold.

Stieglitz insisted they were beautiful but I wasn't so
sure — knobbly knuckles, an unusually long distance
between first and second joints, close-clipped
fingernails, half-moons. But my hands shed light.

We worked, my hands and I. I bound them together
— thin sticks — a raft on which I set desire
and floated downriver toward an unimaginable
destination.

Stieglitz stood on shore and called, *Come back! Come
back! Let me take your picture!* Yet he was always glad
to see what we discovered, my hands and I.

One day I painted each nail a different colour, crossed
my fingers, leaned down and painted my toes.
The floor was orange. I bent forward on all fours
like an animal, tentative at first, finding confidence
in this new balance, new gait, the strength of my arms,
my hands. I knew then — they would hold me.

14.

I'm enjoying his letters so much, learning
    to know him —
sometimes he gets so much of himself into them
that I can hardly stand it.
It's like hearing too much of Ornstein's "Wild Man's
    Fancy" —
you would lose your mind if you heard it twice —
or seeing too much light. You shut your eyes
and put one hand over them
then feel around with the other
for something to steady yourself by.

(found poem)

15.

The thing seems to express in a way what I want it to,
but it also seems rather effeminate —
it is essentially a woman's feeling
satisfies me in a way.
I don't know whether the fault is with the execution
or with what I tried to say.
I've doubted over it
and wondered over it till I had just about decided
it wasn't any use to keep on amusing myself
ruining perfectly good paper trying
to express myself. I wasn't even sure
that I had anything worth expressing.
There are things we want to say
but saying them is pretty nervy.

(found poem)

16.

On the front of a painting
I never wrote my own name
(so full of loops and exclamations).

Instead, if I liked it
if I really liked it,
I turned its face to the wall

and inside a very small star
I printed my initials.
This way, only my friends knew

maybe
that it and I were O.K.

17.

The men painted the shapes they knew —
longer than they were wide —
and no one tripped.

When I painted the shapes I knew —
round hills, dark spaces —
suddenly it was all sex,
the female D.H. Lawrence, orgasmic fountain
on paper at last.
What else would interest the critics
about women?

What made my paintings sell
sickened me.

18.

I had no hands. The men chopped them off when
they saw nothing but sex in my pictures.
There is more to my sex than sex.

They held up their dark, dreary pictures, urged me
to do as they did. I wanted to paint skies and light.

I once heard a story of miners who grew flowers
underground. I wanted to grow them a garden,
though they said it could not be done. Out of darkness,
I would make light.

19.

If I could paint the flower exactly as I see it
no one would see what I see
because I would paint it small like the flower is small.

So I said to myself, I'll paint what I see,
what the flower is to me
but I'll paint it big and they will be surprised
into taking time to look at it.
I will make even busy New Yorkers take time
to see what I see of flowers.

(found poem)

20.

I killed off all sentiment. Did it
for the pictures. It was not allowed
to be an artist and a woman too.
After I joined Stieglitz, there was no question.
My art had sculpted me, made me
the woman you see.
Something round and warm had to go.
What was left were my bones —
terribly beautiful in a hard desert light.

21.

I never told anyone
of my terror of the domestic —
not the housework nor cooking alone
nor even the years spent lost in the kitchen
instead of the studio. No.
My terror was of desperately wanting children.

For years I mourned and begged Stieglitz
but he would not relent. Said it was
too dangerous, saw his sister die
in childbirth, his own daughter
mad with depression afterward.

No, he said. *Take your time, take all your time
and paint. The pictures shall be your children.*

Perhaps he was right.
In the parks of New York I watched children,
the way their mothers took them
for granted with easy glances.
I think now I could not have borne
their noise, leading me to distraction. Still,
sometimes I dream
of a dangerous daughter.

22.

Much as they irritate me
they are all the company I have
(the men, I mean: Stieglitz with his camera,
Paul Strand with his; Dove, Marin and Hartley
with their paints.) And I confess —
sometimes they are a comfort.

Charles Demuth shows me steamy paintings
of men in Turkish baths. We have a bond, he and I.
It is Charles who paints flowers and as I follow
mine grow larger
as if I could hide inside their cropped contours,
as if I could be safe in the silk and fold of petals —
sweet pea, calla and corn.

23.

It's a whiteness, are his words of highest praise
and my favourite clothing is black.
He can't eat the onions I adore.
He hates the thought of children
and I think I might die without one.
He can't stand to be alone
and I crave solitude.
And yet
I adore him.

His sweetness is the thing,
and his stubbornness, matching mine.
That, and without him there would be no
    Georgia O'Keeffe.
Who else adores my discipline
even when it displaces him?
How can I not burn for a man
who, when there is snow, rushes outside
like a child released, to photograph everything,
white waves of it, flakes disappearing in the dark lake,
in love, in love with *white.*

24.

I must find another family. My own will not do.
Mother lived for Father and the children, Father for
himself. I was caretaker to them all. I thought Stieglitz
was different but he takes care of me whether I wish it
or not. He saps and feeds my spirit, both.

I understood this on Friday, sitting in the restaurant
with the men, Stieglitz at the table's head. There was a
moment when he stood and raised his glass and for
one snapshot moment we all adored him, mouths
open, eyes wide to take him in, Alfred Stieglitz, the
wise, the great photographer. And suddenly I knew.
I had found my own family again.

I need another — one that is fatherless. Perhaps a
mother, a woman painter, some kind of kith and kin.

25.

In dreams I pad like an animal through streets
stretched shiny under the bright mica moon.

I am lost and looking for something important,
a question not yet asked —

someone or something is close behind.
We will be together for a while.

I will be still and when she comes,
the moon will make a circle around us,

a single star will shine.

II. NEW MEXICO: LIGHT OVER WATER

When I turned out the light and lay down last night —
I saw a star out the window
Laughed and slept
I wonder if the star was there before and I couldn't see it
                                    — *Georgia O'Keeffe,*
                    in a letter to Elizabeth Stieglitz Davidson

26.

Who is this strange woman
got up like a gunny sack,
smelling of cedar and something else?
An excitement, I smell, that matches my own.

I watch from Stieglitz' broom-closet of an office
as she tours the gallery.
With the men's dark things she is merely polite
but in front of my bright flowers
she stiffens. What does she see?
I am dying to ask, frozen here
in my dark cell, alone
with the critics, including Stieglitz
who sees sex and sales in everything.

What does this strange woman see?
So like me and so different, a string bean and a pea
growing in the same garden.

27.

Under cover of the crowd we tell secrets —
things no one else knows for sure.
Biographers will speculate
for ages.
Each of us grasps for the key
to the other.

In the afternoon we part —
Emily for some other gallery
insisted on by Stieglitz, I, to paint —
each with a tiny icon of the other
pinned carefully over our hearts.
It whispers to me — *Sister.*
We are met at last.

28.

I pack the suitcase, trembling with excitement.
And fear. Alfred will miss me.

He is so fragile, so tragic.
His long white fingers play with my valise,
his eyes cast down in sorrow.

But I must go —
it is for my spirit, for my life.

29.

A dull Sunday.
Emily and I take a walk
in my desert before dinner.

She is one of the few
I have invited
into this space.

I walk fast, head down
looking for a path,
for bones and snakes and pretty rocks.

Emily pokes along on short legs
close to the ground, pointing out shapes
and light, the sky.

She calls me *Albatrosse*. I call her *Mouse*.
We run a close race
tying together heaven and earth.

30.

On our first night in the desert, I dream a large dark
figure approaches me slowly, from far away. Nothing
will stop its coming but I am not in danger. In the
moment before I can say, *It is this*, it begins
to dissolve, flesh fading from bones, huge eyes fixed
on me.

When I wake, I am trembling, gripped by fever,
haunted by the melting of flesh. I make a cup of
bouillon and wrap my hands around hot comfort.
Tonight I miss Stieglitz terribly. Steam rises from
between my hands like the breath of an animal.

On the second night I dream again. This time it is an
animal whose breath is a breeze past my ear, a
whistling like wind through the curve of caves. Its
terrifying passivity demands something of me. On the
third night, I dream again. This beast will wait until I
give it what it yearns for.

The next day I am restless, walk in the desert for
hours. There is something cleansing about a dry high
heat, as if any mist can be burned away. Finally as the
sun sets and I turn to come home, something catches
my eye. It is white — not rock. The skull of a cow.
At last.

31.

She can't see them,
insists
on painting my hills
in shades of British green.
They're everything but! I snap
Try purple! Try yellow! Try red!

She's drenched in green,
bewitched by it. Her eyes
drip curtains of tree colour.
When I am being kind, I think
she's either blind
or homesick.

What is the matter with this woman?
This ground doesn't feed her.
I expect to see her one day
lying prostrate on the yellow earth
face up, tongue out,
sucking the green juice of cactus.

Doesn't she notice the air is clearer here?
Through its crystal curtains
I see the bones of hills.
They shimmer in the heat —
amethyst, ivory and flame.

32.

I take her with me to Taos but
she pines endlessly for forest.
There is no green, she mourns
and stretches her neck
in a most unseemly manner
like a turtle
reaching for water.
I was ready to send her back
till we went to Bandelier
to see the cliff dwellings
and something there arrested her,
held her attention
at last. I was growing tired
of feeding her water and shade.
Now she wants to paint Bandelier
for days at a time.
I feel the spirits here, she says.
There is something speaking
that feels like home.
She has become a woman obsessed.

33.

When I tear her away from Bandelier
we go out in the desert to paint.
As we drive, Emily sees shapes
everywhere, circles and cones.
It frightens me.
I want to hold her hand,
ask her how she does it —
how she stays in a rain forest alone
with sullen shapes that touch her
on the soft flesh at the inside of her elbows,
at the nape of her still, bowed neck.

When I begin to see
hills that loop and crawl, curl
in on themselves — or worse,
reach out — I tell her we must stop,
the sun's too high. I tell her
I can't see at all.

34.

Emily and I watch each other
from the same grey-green eyes,
storms
ready to rise.

We gauge each other's tempest
against an invisible mark.

We watch
from the same grey-green windows, ready
to tear the blinds
off friendship
if the other dares
the slightest.

Honesty being cash for both of us,
we have intrigued, caught up
in the artful pool of the other's passion.
The deal we make
is for this time only.

35.

She is such a prude.
When I paint, I take off my clothes,
let the silk of sunshine run
over my breasts, my thighs,
into my paintings.

Emily is shocked, tells me
it is ungodly,
keeps her eyes cast down
as she doggedly paints hills and houses
while dressed in those potato sacks
she sews for herself.

Even her head is covered. *At least
uncover your eyes!* I say. *Look up!*
The men have never heard me
like this.

36.

On our walks
I hurry her along, fearful
she will notice something private.

I distract her with stories
of the people who drive me crazy
with their talk talk talk.
I tell her about the clutch of women
who came to my gate
in the middle of the desert.

God knows how they found me.
I go there to be lost.
When I answered the knock at the gate
they said, *We want to see Georgia O'Keeffe.*
I said, *Front!* then turned around. *Back!*
Now you've seen her! Good-bye!
and slammed the gate.

Stieglitz gave me hell, told me
I might have got a sale if I hadn't been so rude.
Emily just laughed, that clear bell peal
that opens doors.

37.

Emily is like me.
When we walk the desert there is an empty quality
    to her,
a blank canvas thirsty for filling.

As hunters we track the beast
of colour and shape.
Often she hears it first, like a breath,
a heartbeat (pounding)
closer until we say in one voice:

There! A picture! and laugh
because I am looking up and she
is looking down.

38.

What a ghastly houseguest!
While dressed for an igloo or an icebox
she dares complain about the heat.
When I point this out,
she won't remove a single sensible stocking.

I thought we agreed on one thing —
that we both loved to walk. Now she says
she hates it — always did. Sulks
in my one good chair
dropping her filthy cigarette ashes
on my best woven rugs.
Next thing you know, she'll want to go home.

And I shall miss her. Today she brought me
a Jimson weed flower, told me
not to take her so seriously.
How can I help but love her?
We are fuelled by the same passion, like the Jimson
     weed,
for the same good earth, same sky.

39.

We sit after dinner, one of my finer efforts,
relaxing in front of the fire
while she tells me of meeting Lawren Harris
and the rest of her Canadian Group of Seven.

I have never seen her so animated. She says now
    she dares
to think her art worthwhile after all. I am as amazed
as those men that she ever should have doubted it.

Flames flicker across her face as she talks,
her hands mold structures of green and brown
she will one day paint. I suddenly see
how lucky I have been, knowing Stieglitz
and the men around him.
I am a hothouse flower nourished by their adoration.
Emily has fought like some fierce lonely weed
to find her sun.

I sit back, humbled. My dark eyes reach out to
    touch her.
Lean on me, they say. *Use me.*
Later I cannot remember if I said it aloud.

40.

An impatience burns me.
When I am with her
I am nothing but irritated
by her high round bursts of bustle, intense focus
on trees wherever she can find them.
She wallows in arroyos, clings
with her fat Victorian fingers and toes
to damp valley floors.

She ignores me, fusses over paint,
heedless of the need to watch for snakes
and spiders, dangerous companions.
Hog wash! she says. *They wouldn't dare!*
and won't hear another word about it.
It's only the dogs, I'm sure, who have kept her safe
as she wanders by serpentine water.

When she hides in the cool sulk of the house
I finally escape her, go off by myself for a long walk
or lie on the patio naked, baked clean under the
    hot sun.
Why is it, then, that I miss the hum and gurgle
of her English accent, that sharpness
that spears pomposity and makes me laugh.
Sometimes I can't bear her
being the only one I yearn for.

41.

She's tough,
rants at me worse than the men
for not enough joy,
not enough paint.

More! More! she demands of me
over and over.
*Paint all your life into it
or don't bother painting at all!*

I have gone back to the abstract.
It is the only thing that satisfies her —
openness and movement
around a white hot core.

42.

Last night I dreamed the blood
ran in my veins like skeins of thread,
each thread a different, shimmering colour
as my heart beat scarlet,
chartreuse, cerulean blue.

I awoke knowing that when I am an old woman
I shall live on cactus and thread.

43.

On days like this I hate painting, want to break my
brushes and stalk off, furious, back to the clean lines
of home. Instead, I watch Emily.

Painting trees below the cliff dwellings at Bandelier,
she thinks she is back in her rain forest. Shadows dash
across her face, her body twitches in animate
conversation with that limb, that trunk, that flash
of water down below. She hardly looks at her palette,
dives forward into the space where small pines twist
with wind, burn with light. Emily follows them
to where sap boils. Light and darkness drench her.

I hear her arboreal music, smell perfume — pine.
Emily doesn't paint — she surrenders her paint brush
to the tree. It waltzes with us across a clearing to
where the grandmothers stand, too old to dance but
nodding in dark approval.

Then slowly she returns to centre, breathes a soft
retreat to her camp stool, her palette, me.

When first I met her, I thought her odd-looking and
old. Now I look again. I want to smooth the shadows
from her forehead, paint her beautiful as pine.

44.

Emily talks of Freud.
I hate him.
It was this new man, Freud,
who made them see only sex
in my paintings.

But Emily slows me down,
shows me
the flowering of ribs and pelvis I painted today.
Here is your desire, she says.
See how you have wished it upon paper.
It is a woman's mind, a woman's hand, a woman's
*   voice*
and you didn't even know.
See how it shines from the inside, out.

45.

There is a cauldron between us
part passion
part place.
We snap at each other then separate
to the desert only to rush back
bereft.

Then the small habits of her English propriety,
her yappy dogs, infuriate me all over.
How does she
haunt me?

Body heavy with a strange grace,
her temper grave and radiant
like paint
a dark stroke of fire.

I lean toward her, listening fiercely.
If she is the instrument
I am the song.
We make a syncopated sense.

This Emily echoes in me,
a hum between us, sting
of anticipation.
What will she say?
What will she do?
What will she paint
next?

She is the flint that strikes flame,
flickers between us.
These days I paint
scarlet skies, incinerated plains,
flowers alight and freely burning.

46.

Emily found the perfect rock.
When she set it down
                    and wasn't looking
I took it
of course.
Later she said I stole it but
I hadn't stolen it at all.
It was mine.

Emily says I am even more difficult
to get along with than she is.
That is what makes us friends.
She says she will not be so nice
when we go to British Columbia.
There, everything belongs to her.

47.

This morning we were silly, played
hide-and-seek in the shelter of the patio
like children, hugged the round red
mud of adobe walls patted into place for centuries
by women's hands.

I let her catch me when her hurrying steps touched
the thick dark shadow that trailed me.
She teased, said the sun had made me fat.
Later, she stood bathed in the light
of afternoon.
Georgia! she called, and pointed
to the earth at her feet.

I have drawn her as a thin dark line.
We are now each other's shadow.

48.

We sit in the desert, silent
inside, a single candle
for light. It is the night
before we leave for British Columbia
and I fear what I may find there.
I do not tell her I am afraid.

Emily insists we listen to Bach sonatas — piano and
     cello.
When she puts on the record her hand rises, casts
a gold shadow over black disc.
Usually there is agony in this music, heart aching,
beauty sneaking in with an arrow.
But tonight, music settles me like light over water.
We listen as the strings rise — paint brushes are a
     poor second.

Emily says, *The cello is you, so somber.* She says,
You are the long loosed sob of strings
sliding through colour.

Why not a voice? I ask. *Let me be voice,*
song rising like smoke, meticulous.
But if I am cello, then you are the clear wooden stop
     of piano,
quick press of the keys.

Emily frowns. *I never liked the piano — casket*
with a tight grip, a narrow upright

Christian instrument. Reminds me of the parlour,
stolid old thing, forever prayers and scabby knees
and stolen glances out the window at Sundays.

Don't be silly, I say. I want to make her angry.
You are piano set like wooden seeds
in the earth, to rise, darkly. Emily storms and stomps
   off to bed.
Her boot heels spark lightning on stone.

We are solo instruments, she and I.
We hardly fit. No harmony, so much the like.
I drum my fingers — staccato, accelerando
and watch the candle burn.
It is darker, lonelier without her.
Music continues — a wooden handhold of keys,
a long walk under thin strings of trees.

III. BRITISH COLUMBIA: DUET

A condition of complete simplicity
(Costing not less than everything).
— *T.S. Eliot*

49.

I wake up early on the first day
expecting the bright hot sun and exuberant
insects of New Mexico. Instead
the air is a dull sheen like the light at the back
of a mirror

and there is no sound. No sound at all.
Suddenly I cry, *I am buried alive!*
and only my breath, the sound of my voice
reassures me — I am still alive, in Victoria, in
   British Columbia,
with Emily.

50.

She feels too much and yet
she carries on painting.
I've told myself this is impossible.

Her best friend, Sophie, is an old, ugly Indian
who's lost seventeen babies. Sophie's portrait hangs
on her studio wall.

From cockatoos to cats to rats, she adores animals
and those dozens of dogs.

From where comes this warmth?
She is a hot stove that warms those like her,
who are scorned by others.

Me, I glitter like steel.
She is the only fire that could melt me.

51.

She is poor. I see now why
she paints with house paints and brown paper.
She is a landlady, taxed
to the limits of a temper as short as mine
by the trivia of houseguests.
Yet her work is rich
with a thickness of paint
that makes me look again at my own.

Beside hers, my paintings look as if
someone has strained them through a filter,
as if the painter made a focussed effort to reveal
nothing. I have flattened my own round curves
under a careful glaze of paint
for which the men praise me.
I was pleased they couldn't find
a single brush mark. My canvases are
hairless and sleek, smooth as millponds.

The forms remain thick with a feeling
I can't hide, but the paint lies flattened
as if under glass, untouchable, sealed
from damage
and hurt.
This is a pain I never saw till now,
until I saw Emily's paint
rolling over the canvas, leaving
her thick mark, her woman's finger print.

52.

When we go into her woods together to paint
I don't tell her I am terrified. She is right.
These woods creep, full of shape
and movement that captures me
alive in a too-female place. I drown
in its round spaces, dark edges, wet mirror
of desert mirage, made real.
I know absence rather than plenty.
Our only difference is rain.

53.

I want to grasp the raw wet of her painting
with my two hands, shake out secrets
like pine cones from a ripe tree.

As Stieglitz photographed me
over and over, so I would paint her
as if trying to snag
something not understood
but yearned for.

Perhaps after all,
my muse is not like the men's —
naked and vulnerable,
graceful as a birch —
but sharp and round and crabby, a berry bush
that answers to *Emily*.

54.

This quaint British custom of tea at the Empress
with her sisters, sitting
with knees together impossibly tight and polite.
I can't bear it. Outside a wind howls.

I watch sanctimonious lips wrinkle and droop,
pronouncing in foreign accents I won't understand.
For entertainment, I imagine fat old ladies without
    their clothing on.
Afterward, Emily takes me for a walk in the storm
    with the dogs

in Beacon Hill Park.
It is a wild grassy place, near night, bending under
    the lash
of wind, trees whispering and shushing each other
    on the one side,
ocean caterwauling on the other.

The violence of the water calms me. I can see at last
an open space of sky and stars over desert-flat hills
of ocean and my thoughts
marching boldly before us.

Finally, the waves speak in an accent I can understand.
It is the silence of the desert, made manifest in
    motion.
Winds mourn like coyotes.
The hiss of spray rustles like the dry breath of sage

and the moon drenches us in a pale blue light
that covers my desert, Emily's forest, alike.
When pellets of rain cut me like wind-blown sand
I am startled and laugh aloud, then Emily too

and we yelp and hoot like a sparking fire, alive
under the bright mother moon.

55.

A tedious day of guests pretending to admire
Emily's work but really they were there
because Victoria gossip has already sniffed out
that there's another of those queer
woman painters staying at Hill House —
two in one room at once being too much
for any self-respecting Victorian to ignore.

So over they all prance while the chairs
are hauled down off the ceiling
for this horrible at-home affair.
I don't know why Emily doesn't just keep me
as secret as all the rest of her life.

For our dinner, too exhausted to cook
we settle for an egg and the pale local paste
they call bread, then entertain each other
by listing every name we know they have called us.

Sour, says Emily. *Prickly as a plump little porcupine.*
Eccentric, I match her, *Cranky, unacceptable, crazy.*

All this, we both know, is code for
Be silent. Don't paint.
We laugh till tears run down our faces
till Emily says, *Don't cry* and I realize I can't stop.
It has been so long.

56.

I need — I shall go home.
I see shadows — dark green, mud and brown all over
    her canvas.
Use red! I command her. *Try treason, yellow!*
All that bleakness of green.
Give those forests their space!
Let something bloom!

Forests don't want space, she replies, testy.
They love the dark.

Afterward I wonder why it matters.
They're hers, after all. At least they have life,
green fighting with green.
In memory I haul out my own canvases, have
a private show, watch colour.

In the desert I captured the russet of rock
the black bloom of crosses at sunset but here
in Emily's dark north, I crave only white.
Some of my paintings are flooded with light but white
can also drown things, obliterate them entirely
in glare. Emily thinks my whites say,
Erase me.

Meek and mild, graceful,
I have carved too many pretty shapes for the world,
painted within the lines, polite light.

Tomorrow, far from home, I shall try a different focus,
white with a hint of bone, white blazing, sharp
as a razor.

57.

This afternoon she leaves me alone in her studio
while she visits those Victorian sisters I can not abide.
Finally, alone, I see all her work laid bare.
All afternoon I lay out paintings, pace among them,
hold my thoughts, judge and compare. There is no
   doubt —
Emily is the green motion, green heat of trees.

I am bolder, hold no inhibitions,
but she makes a frank statement
without timidity or evasion, speaks directly
to the senses, nothing vague.
She is *fresh and energetic and fierce and exacting*
and her temper battens my own.

I cannot leave her so long as she paints like this,
like a nun, religious in her commitment
to rhythm and movement and something more,
the pounding of blood in her art.

58.

She pesters me north. Finally I agree — Tofino.
No further.
Bad enough, mile after mile on the back of a wagon
under a green canopy so high it hurts my neck.

She's right. There's a presence here
that spooks me. So many
large live things
implacable, immovable, astute.
Too many. Too large.
No tamed gentility
of Lake George or New England here,
nor the emptiness of Texas.

These trees. These giants. These ghosts
have claimed the land,
the air even, with a damp green
that allows my own small breath
only in the sunlit clearings, which are few.
After the light and dry of desert,
everything here is dark and water.
Abundance drowns me.

Everything is wet: trees, stumps, rocks
are softened into pillows of moss and lichen.
I walk as if through church chambers
of hemlock and cedar, pine, spruce and fir.
Constantly over my shoulder, someone watches me.

I want to shout, "I surrender!"
to the next small precious space of air and light.

I look at firewood differently now,
as living limbs.

When Emily leaves me, I yearn
for a human face. I cling, berating her
for bringing me
to this place of too-large shadows, darkness
at the edge of too much light.

59.

So many days to get in and now
I'm well and truly here. Stuck
in a world of darkness. No maps.
No quick escape. I'm in for it now.

I'm furious, haven't talked to Emily in days.
She's hardly noticed.
Talks all the more to her stupid rat,
the monkey, the dogs.

We are a veritable, if reluctant, family
hunkered down under all these trees
under a scrap of sunlight,
painting. Only one of us
has any bearings.
Only one of us knows any way out.

60.

She has none of my privilege, nor wealth
nor Stieglitz, who fosters my fame,
who made my painting possible —
and yet
I am brittle and thin, starving
for what feeds her.

I rattle with envy that a woman so common, so plain
and so poor should overflow with such wealth.
It drips from her brush like butter.
Her palette is rich with it.

I want what she has.
I know no other way to get it
than to be here, in her forest,
sitting under this damned dripping tree for hours,
trying to see through her eyes
with her.

61.

It's always raining in a rain forest.

This may seem self-evident but I
only grasped it today. There we sat
wrapped in mackintoshes
under the eternal drip,
when I looked up to a perfectly clear blue sky.
Emily caught my motion.
Beautiful day, she said
and grinned
as a steady veil of water fell between us
from the canopy above.

My sketchbooks and even my skin
are swollen in damp.
Wetness is everywhere.
It comes from branches above
and runs in freshets below.
It sits in damp puddles
and rises in mist off the forest floor.
It wets my clothes and hands
as I brush by leaves. Even as I sit,
it lies on my skin like a perpetual sheen
of forest-raised sweat.

In this country, by day I sip the air
and by night I float.

62.

Finally
I have found that if I lie on my back
and look up
I can see sky again, through the narrow spaces
between the needles and leaves of trees.

As this cedar waves in the wind
these spaces smile and blink, open and shut
but I can see blue
and cloud
and light
at last.

Emily laughs
and invites me back to my camp stool
but I refuse.
In New Mexico, I tell her,
I cannot lie on the ground
for fear of snakes and scorpions.
I will stay here just a little longer
with my back to the earth,
making eyes at heaven.

63.

Emily suggests I paint tree trunks
the same way I've painted flowers —
in huge close-ups, nose up against
vast gnarled trunks, bark
I could get lost in, curling limbs.

Terrifying thought.

That would be like walking in
among a herd of brown elephants
saying, *Nice tree, good tree, there now,*
hoping this alone would keep their
scaly trunks at bay.

No, there is a reason I picked flowers.
It's Emily who tames elephants.

64.

When finally we break through the trees,
the sight of ocean pins me to my place.
I am captured by its perfect rhythm.
My heart calms. Vastness at last!
Every evening after a day of painting
under the ominous cackle,
the bitchy gossip of trees,
I run to water lying like mesa,
a table   blue   spreading
a cloth of quiet over my day-trembling ears
a feast of endless open motion for my eyes.

65.

If I were a singer, I would sing in an ocean choir
where the scene overhead hums fog,
the cry of gulls, eagle mew.

Here is a baseline beat of breakers, melody of waves
running glissando to my feet.
Deadheads float like dark notes
scribed on green ledger-lines of sea.
Pebbles in the sand whisper grace notes, ready
and Emily's world is as hushed
as the moment when the conductor raises her arms
and motions us all to begin.

66.

Twenty eight years old and always
a good girl, 1915 marked the break,
the first time I painted for myself
and it was all downhill from there
ending up here, at Emily's feet, in Emily's forest.

When I joined Stieglitz and the men in New York,
I remained abstract so no one knew
the thin cord that tethered me
to the inevitable earth.
I painted flowers, cropped
their anchoring stems, revealed
nothing.

It wasn't until Emily
that I met the ground again —
the texture of bark, the gravity of greens.

Emily has ripped open everything.
Now that I have seen the earth, I lift.
Anchored, I see right through the ribs
of New Mexico's hills
to sky.

67.

Emily has a God, her companion, explanation
for everything. What do I have?

When I am alone in the long dark night, I have
the paintings. No — I have colour. The desert.
Stieglitz.

He stands like a bulwark, lean dark scarecrow
between me and the flapping world. But lately
I yearn to be uninhabited, cloistered, alone.

I dream of becoming a hermit,
growing lush with solitude, indivisible
in exile. Only Emily understands when I say
I yearn to be forsaken.

68.

Everything yearns to be round and yet
she thinks I am beautiful
in this long, lean flesh.
She sees the thinness of my paints
and even that, she loves.
A small round miracle
she makes me believe I can be whole
as a desert skull.

It is all absence and presence.
Stieglitz would never forgive me if I stayed.

Emily tells me I can do this for myself
if I wish it. If I can continue
to be brave.

Ah, but it all takes so much courage —
to be alone, to be connected —
and I am always afraid.

69.

On our return from Tofino by boat
we are lost
in the muted white world of fog,
the sea
a tableland
of so much wet.
My eyes strain until
I close them, wave-blind.
Water scrawls messages
inside my lids, white on black

and sudden as a splash, the boat is surrounded
by shining sea creatures, black and white
with gentle eyes that guide us to the place we seek.
The sun, breaking through,
skitters over grateful waves.

The whales leave with a splash that Emily says
is luck. They give me back my vision.
Now I see why she stays, dissolved
in this world of wetness and water.

70.

Emily is my mother, lover, child.
She does not know this,
that with her,
I break the bonds
of the demon that rides me
to perfection.
With her I can be
merely Georgia —
this name, this body,
this mother, this lover,
this child.

71.

She says if I lay my head against a tree
in a storm
I will hear a vibrating chord.
It is the drone of storm, she says.
The forest sings with it.

Someday I shall tell her
that the desert too, clamours and wails
a streak of shining mica.

I shall tell her the desert is a diva
laced with veins, schists
in violet, sienna and gold
under a pale ochre skin.

This is what I yearn to paint —
>   *She* who is terrifying
>   *She* who is buried
>   *She* who fills your mouth with ash

wind over mesa, the song of her weeping.

72.

My job has been to build a barricade
between me and everyone else

except Stieglitz
and lately him too.

I took love where I could find it
from men, women, my husband.

I was tight and contained
until Emily mined me through.

Now I spill like a waterfall.
A river has found its way through me.

With her, I spew words, theories, praise
swallow her up, thirsty

for the flow of another painter who thinks
in a body like mine.

In each other's presence
we are changelings.

It shall be our secret
lest others make us explain.

On this one thing, we agree.
We have made a pact

never to speak of this meeting.

IV. INWARD TO THE BONES

She hides her heart
so she can walk in the desert
She draws her sex in the sand
and waits for darkness

Oculta su corazon
para caminar en el desierto
Dibuja su sexo en la arena
y espera la oscuridad

— Myriam Moscona,
Una Mujer

73.

Emily follows me
even here, even now.
Black hills are carved
to look like the skirts of
her endless trees.

She will know it is the forest
that hid me, follows me.
It is all a blackness
above the bracken and the unknown.

We never talked of tornadoes or lightning
but they're here too.
I should have known —
we've started something.

And the paint flows. I can't help it.
As if an impossible rain, as if just
the thought of her breathes turpentine
over my palette. Green conundrum
in a dry place.

74.

March 2, 1945

I wake up in the night at the hour when the moon
   comes round
and I know.

Emily sits at the foot of my bed.
It's been so long, I say,
as if I am not surprised after all these years
to see her impatient in her hair net
and self-created flour-sack gown.

She has come to say good-bye. She's not joking this
   time.
For a moment I feel her presence with only a hint of
   prickle,
as it was all those years ago when no one knew.
What she gave me then is mine forever.
Goodbye mouse, I say to the darkness.

A light wind shifts the sheet —
a grey bird lifts.

75.

Now people ask me if I don't get lonesome,
alone in the desert for days at a time.
Dumb question.

If I needed merely words, I would be bound
to my unforthcoming neighbours. Living alone,
even the speaking of my name is an interruption.

Instead, I have emerald, indigo, red.
Along my adobe walls, canvases stand like ghosts
waiting their turn to come in
to the brilliant conversation of colours.

76.

Fierce in red and white and black
I am insignificant but tell no one that.

I fit the folds of these warped hills
like an animal its skin.

Mongoose, lizard, snake
like these rejected ones

I make the mark of three —
Emily, the desert, me.

77.

There are no sundials here.
I will not allow them. My favourite place
is in the hot sun at noon, alone, lost but not lost
like one of those dark creatures
that lived under bridges in my grandfather's
Hungary.

I am one thin line. You cannot see behind me —
no trace, no clue. Nothing to know about me.
Wicked woman, you say,
solitary stalk who dares grow in her own garden,
solitary black bird in a perfectly blank sky,
only woman
in a world of desert and men. Regardless
I have stood: dark, straight, shadowless.

78.

Dressed in black, I stalk desert
        sharp eyes piercing the distance.
I will tear what I want from this place —
        vistas, views, colour.
I will eat its bones.

The locals call me crazy, white woman in the black coat
        white flesh, black bones.
I track the shape of hills with a woman's body
        that swallows colours whole.

On another hot desert day I circle
        look for what feeds my art.
Today especially, I look for fellowship —
        seek out birds of prey.

79.

I want to cut sharper, deeper
to the marrow
and people just want more flowers. These days
I throw in the private joke of a blossom or two.

Heat and silence and space are the drugs I use
to travel closer
to the heart of things.
It was Emily taught me this,
to look inward, to the bones.
They are so alive.

80.

When I paint certain things
I try not to imagine
the thought within them.
I have always done this but more
as I grow old. Perhaps because
the thought grows more complex
with age, and sometimes ugly.

Some pictures, the thought crowds the thing until
you wouldn't recognize the plain earth of it
for the vast thought that bares it.
I'm always embarrassed
at how literal such portraits are
and shocked when people don't see them.

Now, I make the pictures simple,
leave my thoughts aside
so people will not be upset with the paintings,
with me. It is easier this way
and I sell more.

81.

The renovations to my new house in the desert
proceed according to plan.
By day the women smooth every inch
of the red earth adobe
with their bare hands
as they have done for centuries.
Round walls and many windows for light —
this is a woman's house.

But each night, surrounded by wreckage, I dream
I am in my father's house again, my husband's
footsteps echoing,
ghostly imprints shimmering behind me show
where I have been.
But in this dream I am lost.
Where do I go from here?
Where is my map?
That is the house I did not build

and only now do I allow myself
to leave that one, for this other.

82.

Fall arrives,
the season of darkness. Now at last
the tourists leave
and I am alone in the desert
where night comes early.

The air is brilliant as I perch
on a thin lip of rock.
I wear darkness, black
as a crow
          eyes bright.
Shadow is the place
that interests me.
Under these dark wings
I hide my stubborn bones.

I look for breaks in the light, bodies
of shape or colour, stone or sand —
everything is a model for my eye, my hand
the paint.

I am never tentative,
strike fast and deep.
My eyes pry open light and dark
and meaning. The rest of the time
I am silent as a bird of prey
hunting images that thrill me.

My Buddhist neighbours say,
We are love or we are fear
but I am neither, hover
in the middle, pinned tight
to my solitary nourishment.

83.

Now my eyes begin to go.
At first I used other people's eyes,
telling them what to do, what shapes.
In ceremonies of paint,
wafers of colour passed on my tongue.
It was a pallid communion.

Three months ago a young man came to my door.
He did the odd jobs, minded
garden and dogs, washed windows, but lately
he amuses me with the sharpness
of his conversation, his care.
I told him one day to show me
how he makes pots. He touched my hands,
guided me to wet hills of clay.
For this I need no sight. The ten senses of my fingers
mold globes round
as a desert hill, a woman's belly.

I love these pots, know their colours
by heart. His name is Juan Hamilton.
Together we make love
to the round forms of clay and country.

84.

Bone to bone,
I am embedded now
in this land

deep as a tick on a mangy old dog.
No matter how hard you scratch

you can't budge me now.
I shall die here, hot

and clean, finally
the faraway nearby.

85.

My skin was marked by the typhoid pox.
I ignored it, refused to hide behind make-up
but I made the skin of my canvas
smooth under paint
so no defect showed.

As a child I was hidden away, but my paintings
now hang in front parlours. My children,
my beautiful children, are allowed in the living room
at last.

86.

This space is not emptiness.
This space is not, as you would say, *Nothing there*.
It is a space of fullness, open
to possibility. You would say *A foolish space*.
Perhaps.

Broad in the sense of drawing breath
(that bone-creaking opening)
deep in the sense of well water.
This is not denial. This is joy,
an empty palette waiting, bone
against the sky.
We are so afraid of the larger space.

I know everything from the inside out —
hills, bones, bodies. It is why
I have a hard time seeing people.
They will almost never stand aside.
Only Stieglitz. Emily. Me. I count on one hand
the vaulted ones, the ones who are filled
with the same large space.

87.

I dream a wild wind over my bare bones,
a terrifying song through the cavities of my skull,
my hips. The thin digits of what once were
articulating fingers, trail paint.

I am reduced to light   wind.
I can feel myself inside this body
like hills, like a vaulted room,
like spans or poles set
bone-deep in pearly earth.

A dark shell falls away, light rising
through translucent flesh.
I am haunted by skeletons, stripped clean
of blood and dirt.
Shaken, I vibrate to the sensations
that were once this body. The wind whistles
music through these bones.

AFTERWORD

Art is a wicked thing. It is what we are.
— *Georgia O'Keeffe*

… I discovered that by running against the wind
with a bunch of pine branches in your hand
you could have the pine trees singing
right in your ears…

(found poem)

NOTES ON THE POEMS

2.

In 1906, Georgia O'Keeffe (1887-1986) fell ill with typhoid fever. Although it was unnoticeable on black and white film, her skin from this time on always bore the pitted traces of her sickness. (Benita Eisler, *O'Keeffe & Stieglitz: An American Romance*. NY: Doubleday, 1991, p. 25.) I've taken liberties here with the date, suggesting it happened much earlier.

3.

"I had a whole family of small china dolls — the largest about three inches tall...In time I made a house for the dolls...It was made of two thin boards about eighteen by twenty-four inches. I sawed a slit a little over halfway up each board, then I could fit the slit of one board into the slit of the other and make a house of four rooms...In the summer I took the dollhouse outdoors to a shady place between some hemlock and apple trees and arranged a park to go with the house. I cut the grass with scissors, left weeds tall for trees, made walks with sand and little stones, had a large pan of water for a lake with moss on the edge of it." (Georgia O'Keeffe, *Georgia O'Keeffe*. NY: Penguin, 1988, no page numbers.)

4.

Found poem from O'Keeffe, *Georgia O'Keeffe*.

5.

From an early age, Georgia O'Keeffe defied current fashions for women by dressing in a simple — even severe — style (eschewing ruffles and bows), and almost entirely in black, with white touches.

6.

In the summer of 1912, O'Keeffe took a class at the University of Virginia from Alon Bement who taught the principles of Arthur Wesley Dow (with whom O'Keeffe later studied). Dow's principles were revolutionary but simple. As O'Keeffe explained them, "He had an idea that interested me…the idea of filling a space in a beautiful way. Where you have the windows and door in a house. How you address a letter and put on the stamp. What shoes you choose and how you comb your hair." (Georgia O'Keeffe, *Georgia O'Keeffe*.) Dow also emphasized "the importance of the Japanese concept of *notan*, the balanced values of darks and lights, as the basis of his compositional system." (Charles C. Eldredge, *Georgia O'Keeffe: American and Modern*. New Haven: Yale University Press, 1993, p. 161.)

7.

Found poem in O'Keeffe, *Georgia O'Keeffe*.

8.

In 1917, at the time of the white walls and "square of black cloth" incident, Georgia was teaching in Canyon, Texas. (Eisler, *O'Keeffe & Stieglitz,* p. 154.) In June 1918, she accepted Stieglitz' offer to come live — and paint — in New York. Alfred Steiglitz (1864-1946) ran a series of galleries from which he introduced abstract art to North America. He is known as the "father" of modern photography.

9.

O'Keeffe told an interviewer, "I'm frightened all the time. Scared to death. But I've never let it stop me. Never!" (May Lynn Kotz, "A Day with Georgia O'Keeffe," *ARTnews*, December 1977, in Roxana Robinson, *Georgia O'Keeffe: A*

Life. NY: Harper & Row, 1989, p. 166.) In 1976 she wrote, "I believe that to create one's own world in any of the arts takes courage." (O'Keeffe, *Georgia O'Keeffe*.) At another time, she asked her friend Anita Pollitzer, "Is there such a word as freeest?" She was a notoriously bad speller.

10.

In 1915, O'Keeffe wrote to her friend Anita Politzer, "Self-control is a wonderful thing — I think we must even keep ourselves from feeling too much — often — if we are going to keep sane and see with a clear unprejudiced vision." (Georgia O'Keeffe to Anita Politzer before October 16, 1915, in the Collection of American Literature, Beinecke Rare Book and Manuscript Library, Yale University, New Haven. In Robinson, *Georgia O'Keeffe: A Life*, pp. 119-120.)

11.

Found poem by Georgia O'Keeffe in a letter from O'Keeffe to Anita Pollitzer from Charlottesville, Virginia, summer 1916, in *A Woman on Paper: Georgia O'Keeffe. The Letters and Memoir of a Legendary Friendship* by Anita Pollitzer (NY: Touchstone, Simon & Schuster, 1988, pp. 141-142).

13.

When O'Keeffe first moved to New York in 1918, she stayed in the studio of Stieglitz' niece, Elizabeth Stieglitz. The walls there were yellow, the floor, orange. Soon after she moved in, Alfred left his wife, Emmeline, and moved into the tiny studio with her. It was here that he began his famous series of often nude, portrait photographs of O'Keeffe.

14.

Found poem by Georgia O'Keeffe in letter to Anita Pollitzer

from Canyon, Texas in the fall of 1916. From Pollitzer, *A Woman on Paper*, p. 148.

15.
Found poem in a letter from Georgia O'Keeffe to Anita Pollitzer, Columbia, South Carolina, January 4, 1916. From Pollitzer, *A Woman on Paper,* pp. 120-121.

16.
O'Keeffe neither signed nor gave titles to most of her works.

17.
In 1909, Sigmund Freud visited the United States and gave a major boost to theories of psychology and personality. From the beginning — but particularly after Stieglitz exhibited his intimate portraits of her — critics (including Stieglitz) saw O'Keeffe's work as primarily erotic, revealing "woman." This infuriated and hurt O'Keeffe and she denied it all her life, insisting, "I am not a woman painter." The men she refers to were a circle of young artists and photographers who first called themselves "The Round Table." They revolved around Stieglitz and his weekly lunches. The circle included Arthur Dove, Paul Strand, John Marin, Marsden Hartley, Charles Demuth and, later, O'Keeffe — the sole woman.

19.
Found poem in O'Keeffe, *Georgia O'Keeffe*.

21.
The question of children was a significant and difficult one between O'Keeffe and Stieglitz for some time. O'Keeffe once said she thought she would "die" if she couldn't have a child. Though it is true that Steiglitz' sister died in childbirth and

his daughter (by Emmeline) never recovered from the depression precipitated by giving birth, it is probably likewise true that Stieglitz, who was twenty-three years older than O'Keeffe, wasn't keen on having a baby for personal reasons. He always demanded that he be the centre of everyone's attention.

23.

This incident happened at the Stieglitz' family summer home at Lake George on Sunday, November 25, 1923. (Eisler, *O'Keeffe and Stieglitz*, p. 314). The year before, O'Keeffe had written about Stieglitz to their mutual friend, the writer Sherwood Anderson, saying, "The sweetness of the man is the thing to take hold of." (Eisler, *O'Keeffe and Stieglitz*, p. 288.)

26.

Georgia O'Keeffe and Emily Carr met at the Alfred Stieglitz gallery, An American Place, in April 1930 when Carr was on a trip to New York. Carr briefly recorded the meeting, saying she saw and liked some of O'Keeffe's work, especially *Lawrence Pine Tree, with Stars* (also called *The D.H. Lawrence Tree.)* She also notes seeing and being moved by the works of Arthur Dove. (*Emily Carr*, Doris Shadbolt. Vancouver: Douglas & McIntyre, 1990, p. 62; and *Emily Carr: A Biography*, Maria Tippett. Toronto: Oxford, 1979, p. 175.)

28.

In 1929, for the first time, O'Keeffe left Stieglitz to spend the summer painting in and around Taos, New Mexico. For almost every year after that, including 1930, she did the same. Stieglitz' died in 1946 and in 1949 O'Keeffe moved permanently to Ghost Ranch and then a second home in Abiquiu, near Taos, New Mexico.

43.

Both women loved trees. O'Keeffe once said, "If only people were trees, I might like them better," (Eisler, *O'Keeffe and Stieglitz*, p. 358); and Carr said, "I love trees better than people." (*Hundreds and Thousands: The Journals of Emily Carr*. Toronto: Clarke, Irwin, 1978, pp. 326-327.)

46.

This is based on an event that happened between O'Keeffe and Eliot Porter, the photographer. O'Keeffe collected rocks and when Porter found a very beautiful one while visiting her in the desert, she claimed it. Porter still managed to take it home for his wife. When O'Keeffe later visited him, he left it out as a test — and, sure enough, O'Keeffe took it.

48.

O'Keeffe loved music and several of her early abstractions are "of" music. In 1946 she said, "Singing has always seemed to me the most perfect means of expression. Since I cannot sing, I paint." (Eldredge, *Georgia O'Keeffe*, p. 215). She joked about being reborn as a blonde soprano (Ibid., p. 168). At different times in her life she played piano and violin and one of her favourite pieces of music was Pablo Cassals (on cello) playing Bach. Both O'Keeffe and Carr carefully read Wassily Kandinsky's book, *Concerning the Spiritual in Art* (trans. M.T.H. Sadler, NY: Dover Publications, 1977, first published in 1911). Kandinsky thought painting should aspire to express an "inner" spiritual harmony and that it could learn much from music. He equated the expression of colour and form in abstract painting with that of musical sound.

50.

After O'Keeffe had a nervous collapse in 1933, a friend said she was harder than ever, that she "glitters like steel." (Eisler in *O'Keeffe and Stieglitz*, p. 448.)

51.

O'Keeffe's work, when seen in the original, is noteworthy for its smooth, burnished surfaces. A friend and influential critic of the time, Henry McBride, observed about her work that it seemed "wished upon the canvas — the mechanics have been so successfully concealed." (Henry McBride, January 14, 1933 in Eldredge, *Georgia O'Keeffe*, p. 200.)

For fourteen years — from 1913 to 1927 — Emily Carr kept a boarding house (Hill House) in Victoria, British Columbia. She despised doing this, but it was her only way of making a living. She was so poor that she couldn't afford canvas and experimented with painting with house paints on paper.

55.

These are only some of the epithets applied to these two artists in their time. O'Keeffe's work was also criticized for being "bodiless" and "passive."

56.

In 1928, writing to Henry McBride, O'Keeffe complained about Lake George, "Everything is very green. I look around and wonder what one might paint — nothing but greens." (Eldredge, *Georgia O'Keeffe*, p. 196.)

57.

"Fresh and energetic and fierce and exacting" is Georgia O'Keeffe's description of what she most liked about one of her own important early teachers, William Merritt Chase.

64.

Earlier in her life, when she stayed on the Atlantic coast with friends, O'Keeffe reported with delight that she had gone down to the beach every night.

66.

It was in 1915 that O'Keeffe, teaching in isolation at Columbia College in Columbia, South Carolina, discarded old mannerisms and began a daring new series of abstractions that were a turning point in her career. She sent them to Anita Pollitzer, who showed them to Stieglitz. He is said to have exclaimed when he saw them, "Finally, a woman on paper!" O'Keeffe was then twenty-eight years old.

68.

"I look at what I've done and fear for myself — in an odd way — because it's mine and isn't quite like other things — Always a feeling of walking too near the edge of something." (Georgia O'Keeffe in a letter to Ettie Stettheimer from Ghost Ranch, New Mexico, October 12, 1945. Quoted in Eldredge, *Georgia O'Keeffe*, p. 161, footnote.)

72.

O'Keeffe had, or is strongly suspected to have had, affairs with numerous women as well as men. See Eisler, *O'Keeffe & Stieglitz* and Jeffrey Hogrefe, *O'Keeffe: The Life of an American Legend* (NY: Bantam, 1992).

73.

This poem is based on the painting, "Black Place II, 1944." The area O'Keeffe referred to as the Black Place was 150 miles from Ghost Ranch. It was one of her favourite places to paint.

74.

Emily Carr died March 2, 1945 in Victoria, British
Columbia, fifteen years after this imaginary "journey" took
place.

79.

In 1939, O'Keeffe said about her paintings of bones in the
desert, "the bones are as beautiful as anything I know. To me
they are strangely more living than the animals walking
around…The bones seem to cut sharply to the center of
something that is keenly alive on the desert." (Eldredge,
Georgia O'Keeffe, p. 201.) She began painting them in 1930,
the year I imagine her with Emily Carr.

80.

"I have painted portraits that to me are almost photographic.
I remember hesitating to show the paintings, they looked so
real to me. But they have passed into the world as abstractions
— no one seeing what they are." (Georgia O'Keeffe, 1976.
Quoted in Eldredge, *Georgia O'Keeffe*, p. 173.)

81.

After years of negotiating with the Catholic Church, O'Keeffe
bought a tumbled-down house that was then serving as a pig
pen in Abiquiu, sixteen miles from Ghost Ranch, near Taos,
New Mexico. She ordered extensive renovations, including
large windows that looked out over the valley in front.
Thanks largely to Stieglitz' canny handling of sales of her art,
money was no object.

83.

John "Juan" Bruce Hamilton began working as a handyman
for O'Keeffe in the early 1970s. He fairly quickly became her

permanent companion. When she died in 1986 at the age of ninety-eight, she named him executor of her will and heir to most of her estate.

84.
"From the Faraway Nearby" is the name of one of O'Keeffe's better-known desert paintings, of a fully antlered deer skull suspended in a clear blue sky against distant red hills.

87.
"I can feel myself on the inside of this body like the hills, like a vaulted room, like spans or poles … "
— Susan Griffin, from "Cradles of Light" from *Erotic Interludes: Tales Told By Women* edited by Lonnie Barbach. (NY: Perennial Library, Harper & Row, 1986, p. 247).

Afterword
Found poem, letter from Georgia O'Keeffe to Anita Pollitzer, from Canyon, Texas, October 5, 1916. (Pollitzer, *A Woman on Paper*, p. 151.)

PHOTOGRAPH BY JOHN STEEVES

Kate Braid was born in Calgary, Alberta. She has worked as a receptionist, secretary, child care worker, teacher, lumber piler and carpenter. For several years, she was the Director of the Labour Program at Simon Fraser University. She has taught Creative Writing at the University of British Columbia, Simon Fraser University and Malaspina University-College, and in 1997 she completed her masters degree in Creative Writing. Currently, Braid is a teacher and researcher, and member of the writers' groups "SexDeathandMadness" and "Girls with Day Jobs."

Kate Braid has numerous publication credits including two previous books of poetry, *To This Cedar Fountain* (Polestar, 1995) and *Covering Rough Ground* (Polestar, 1991). The latter book won the prestigious Pat Lowther Award. Braid has also published in journals and anthologies, including *The Malahat Review*, *This Magazine*, *Tradeswoman*, *Room of One's Own*, *East of Main* (Pulp Press), *If I Had a Hammer* (Papier Mâché Press), *Line Work* (Harbour) and *More Than Our Jobs* (Arsenal Pulp Press).

Kate Braid lives in Burnaby, British Columbia.

Whylah Falls • by **George Elliott Clarke**
Clarke writes from the heart of Nova Scotia's Black community. Winner of the
Archibald Lampman Award for poetry.
0-919591-57-4 • $14.95 CAN / $12.95 USA

Prose:
Fresh Tracks: Writing the Western Landscape • edited by **Pamela Banting**
Acclaimed writers **Rudy Wiebe**, **Lorna Crozier**, **Di Brandt**, **Guy Vanderhaeghe**,
Sharon Butala, **Karen Connolly** and more than 30 others explore landscape and
human connection to the western landscape in this provocative collection of
creative non-fiction, memoirs, stories, poetry and song lyrics.
1-896095-42-9 • $21.95 CAN / $18.95 USA

*Sitting in the Club Car Drinking Rum and Karma Kola: A Manual of
Etiquette for Ladies Crossing Canada by Train* • by **Paulette Jiles**
This elegant, quirky work of detective travel fiction has become a cult classic.
This is a special 10th Anniversary edition.
0-919591-13-2 • $12.95 CAN / $10.95 USA

West by Northwest: British Columbia Short Stories
edited by **David Stouck** and **Myler Wilkinson**
A brilliant collection of short fiction that celebrates the unique landscape and
literary culture of BC. Includes stories by **Bill Reid**, **Ethel Wilson**, **Wayson
Choy**, **George Bowering**, **Evelyn Lau**, **Shani Mootoo** and others.
1-896095-41-0 • $18.95 CAN / $16.95 USA

What's True, Darling • by **M.A.C. Farrant**
The first stories in this remarkable collection peel away stardom to expose the
absurdly commonplace; in the second set, "ordinary" people reveal extraordinary
quirks.
1-896095-28-3 • $16.95 CAN / $14.95 USA

Polestar titles are available from your local bookseller.
For a copy of our catalogue, contact:

Polestar Book Publishers
PO Box 5238, Station B
Victoria, British Columbia
Canada   V8R 6N4
http://mypage.direct.ca/p/polestar/